ALEXANDRIAN LIBRARY
MORO OF ALEXANDRIA

ALEXANDRIAN LIBRARY
MORO OF ALEXANDRIA

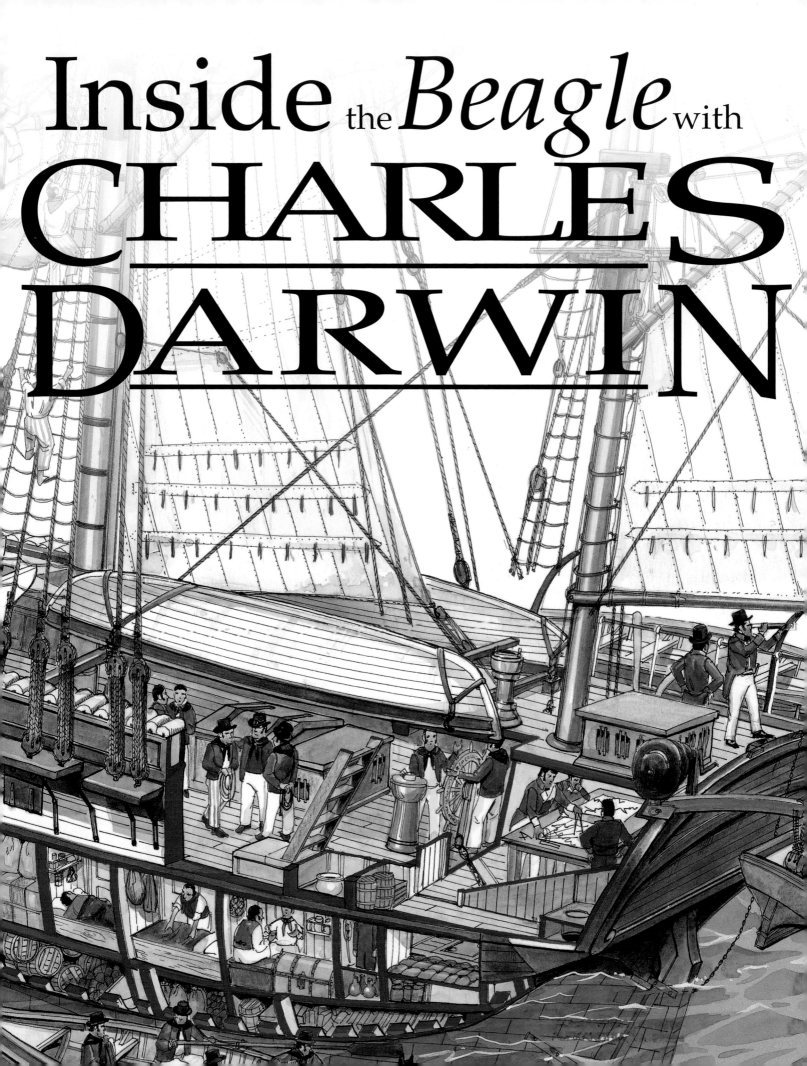

Inside *the Beagle* with

CHARLES DARWIN

First American edition published in 2005 by
Enchanted Lion Books
115 West 18 Street, 6th floor
New York, NY 10011

© The Salariya Book Company Ltd MMV

All rights reserved. No part of this book may be reproduced,stored in a retrieval system or transmitted in any form or by any means, electronic, mechanical, photocopying, recording or otherwise, without the written permission of the copyright owner.

ISBN 1-59270-041-1

Catalog-in-Publishing Data is on file with the Library of Congress

Author:
Fiona Macdonald studied History at Cambridge University and at the University of East Anglia. She has taught over many years, and has written many books on historical topics, mainly for children.

Artist:
Mark Bergin was born in Hastings, England, in 1961. He studied at Eastbourne College of Art and has specialized in historical reconstructions, aviation and maritime subjects since 1983. He lives in Bexhill-on-Sea with his wife and three children.

Series Creator:
David Salariya was born in Dundee, Scotland. He has illustrated a wide range of books and has created and designed many new series for publishers both in the UK and overseas. In 1989, he established The Salariya Book Company. He lives in Brighton with his wife, illustrator Shirley Willis, and their son Jonathan.

Editor: **Michael Ford**

Due to the changing nature of Internet links, the Salariya Book Company has developed an online list of websites related to the subject of this book. This site is updated regularly. Please use this link to access the list:
http://www.book-house.co.uk/inside/beagle

Printed and bound in China. Printed on paper from sustainable forests.

Photographic credits
t=top b=bottom c=center l=left r=right

The Art Archive: 25, 27
The Art Archive / Bibliothèque des Arts Décoratifs Paris / Dagli Orti (A): 43
The Art Archive / South Australia Art Gallery: 18
Mary Evans Picture Library: 8, 30, 42
Mountain High maps / copyright 1993 Digital Wisdom Inc: 6/7, 20, 24, 26, 34/5, 37
© National Maritime Museum, London: 19
Every effort has been made to trace copyright holders. The Salariya Book Company apologizes for any unintentional omissions and would be pleased, in such cases, to add an acknowledgement in future editions.

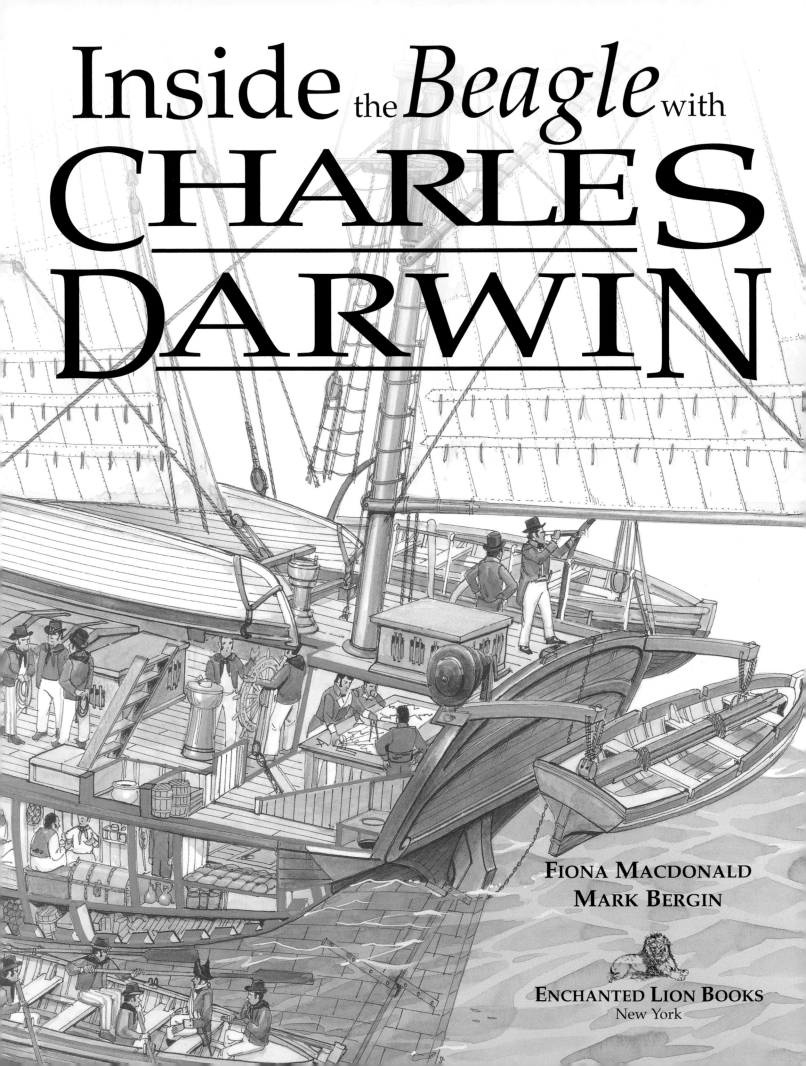

Inside the *Beagle* with
CHARLES
DARWIN

FIONA MACDONALD
MARK BERGIN

ENCHANTED LION BOOKS
New York

CONTENTS

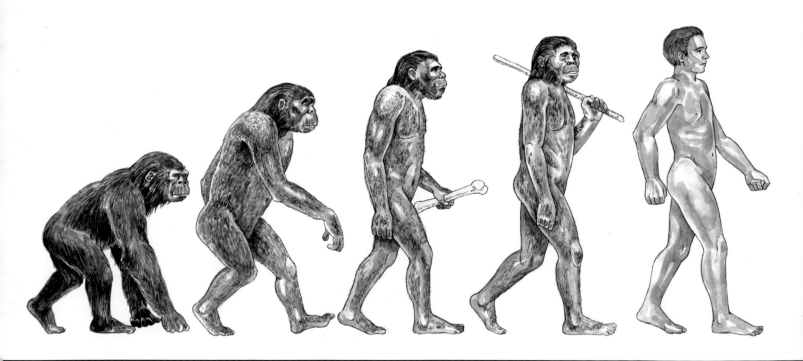

INTRODUCTION

Charles Robert Darwin (1809-1882) began his career as a failure. He had hoped to train for a medical career. But at university he could not face cutting up dead bodies or taking part in brutal surgery, so he left, and studied to become a Church of England priest. However, he did not look forward to a life serving the Church, and instead spent his study time shooting birds, collecting rocks and beetles, and reading about politics and philosophy.

Darwin's life changed forever in 1831. That year he was unexpectedly offered the job of "naturalist" on the *Beagle*, a small sailing ship set for a voyage around the world. Restless, curious and rather bored, Darwin eagerly accepted. On the long voyage Darwin saw sights and collected specimens that would keep him thinking, studying and writing for the next 50 years.

By the time Darwin died he was Britain's most respected scientist. His discoveries challenged religious beliefs and overturned earlier theories. His new ideas—known as Evolution (page 42) and Natural Selection (page 38)—revolutionized the way people thought about the world and understood human nature. They transformed the study of plants, rocks, fossils and societies. They laid down the foundations for exciting new sciences, such as genetics and microbiology, and they still influence scientists today.

A GREAT OPPORTUNITY

Captain Robert Fitzroy of the British Navy was a man of strong character, strange opinions and bold ideas. In 1828, when just a young lieutenant, he had taken command of a navy survey ship, HMS *Beagle,* after its captain went mad and shot himself. Fitzroy completed the *Beagle*'s planned survey of South America, then steered her safely back to Britain in 1830. He brought four Native South Americans back with him, hoping they would learn British ways of farming, and then return home to grow food for British ships sailing past the tip of South America.

The next year, 1831, Captain Fitzroy planned a second voyage in the *Beagle.* He had to continue his survey work for the Navy, and hoped to help the four indigenous people set up their new farms. Fitzroy also wanted to take a "well-educated and scientific person" with him. He realized that the *Beagle*'s voyage would be a great opportunity to investigate wildlife and the environment, as on his first voyage he had seen many plants and animals he did not recognize. So Fitzroy asked the head of Navy surveys to look for a suitable scientist, and he wrote to professors at Cambridge University, who suggested a bright young student, called Charles Darwin.

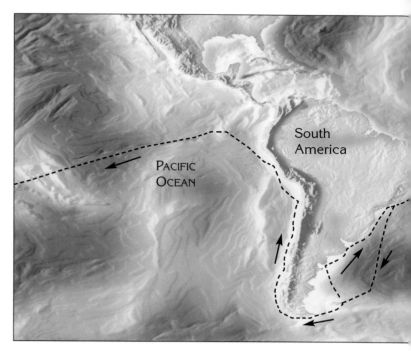

Darwin first met Fitzroy in September 1831. They liked each other. But Fitzroy almost refused to take Darwin on the planned voyage because of the shape of his nose! (It was small.) Fitzroy believed he could tell character from peoples' faces. He thought Darwin did not look energetic or determined.

The *Beagle*'s second voyage began in 1831. Fitzroy was in command, and Darwin was the ship's scientist. They had orders to complete the survey of South America's coastline, then to sail westwards round the world, taking accurate measurements of time. They finally returned home in 1836 after five years at sea.

THE LIFE OF YOUNG DARWIN

Darwin was born in 1801 in Shropshire, England. His father was a wealthy doctor.

His mother came from the famous Wedgwood family. They owned pioneering new factories.

Darwin's father did not want him to join the *Beagle.* He wanted him to become a priest.

Darwin's uncle, Josiah Wedgwood, wrote to persuade Darwin's father to let him sail.

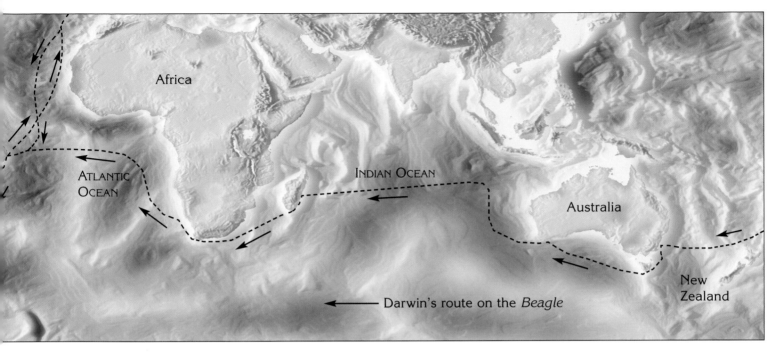

Africa

ATLANTIC OCEAN

INDIAN OCEAN

Australia

New Zealand

← — Darwin's route on the *Beagle*

Microscope

Charles Darwin meeting Captain Fitzroy

Pistols and cleaning equipment

Straight after his meeting with Fitzroy, Darwin began to prepare for the voyage. He found lodgings in London and went shopping for clothes, books, drawing equipment, compasses, a telescope and a pair of pistols.

SHIPS FOR SURVEYING

By 1820, when HMS *Beagle* was launched, Britain had the strongest Navy in the world. Navy vessels patrolled seas all round the globe, protecting Britain from enemy invasion and guarding cargo ships sailing to British ports. These ships carried imported foods such as Chinese tea and Caribbean sugar, and raw materials, such as cotton from India, for Britain's fast-developing factories. The Navy also protected passenger ships carrying emigrants to North America and merchants travelling to British-run lands in India. But to do its job well, and avoid shipwrecks, the Navy needed up-to-date charts of the sea-bed and maps of hazardous coastlines. It also needed accurate information about ocean winds, waves and weather.

HMS *Beagle* was one of six new ships built for the British Navy between 1817 and 1820. All were designed to carry the "Corps of Surveying Officers"—well-trained Navy men who made surveys of seas and coast-lines. These Navy surveyors kept careful records of all they observed and brought them back to Britain. This information was passed on to the Navy Hydrographic Office, where expert draughtsmen (skilled artists) and printers prepared accurate, detailed maps and charts for British sailors to use in peacetime and in war.

HMS *Beagle* was a small, fast sailing ship of 235 tons. It was 90 feet long and 24 1/2 feet wide. Its hull was 12 1/2 feet deep, from the deck to the keel. Originally it carried 8 or 10 cannon for defense. It also carried three smaller boats. One was stored above deck, two hung over the side rails. They were used to survey shallow water, load food and drink, and carry crew members ashore.

A plan of the *Beagle* from 1832

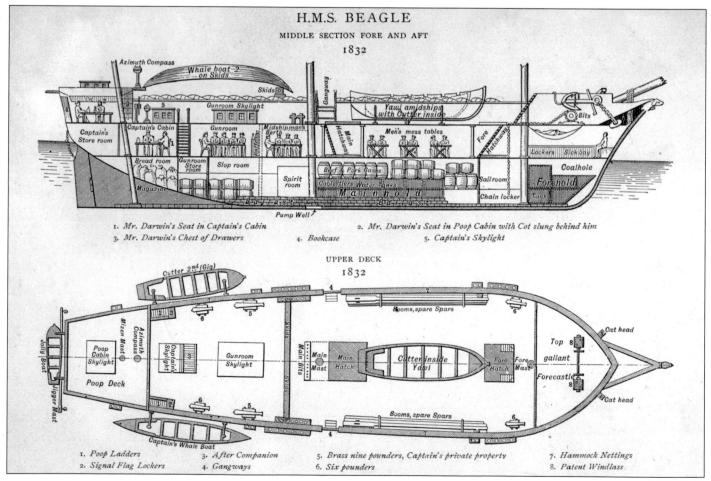

Before the Corps of Surveying Officers was set up in 1817, British sailors had few good maps or charts to help them. They bought the best they could find from chart-sellers in London, but these had many gaps, and were full of dangerous mistakes.

REFITTING AT PLYMOUTH

HMS *Beagle* was built at Woolwich in London, and launched in May 1820. Made of wood, she cost the Navy £7,803 (equal to around $14 million today). For the first five years of her life, the *Beagle* stayed in dock, as a reserve. But in 1825 the Navy got her ready for her first voyage. The hull was covered with thin sheets of copper, to protect it from wood-eating worms found in tropical seas. The main deck was re-built, and a new mast and rigging were added.

The *Beagle* set sail in 1826 and, in her three years at sea, took a terrible battering. By the time Fitzroy planned a second voyage with Darwin on board, she badly needed repairs. In September 1831 Fitzroy and Darwin made eager plans for this new expedition. Full of excitement, they hurried by boat to Plymouth, where the *Beagle* was being re-fitted. But at first sight of the ship in dock, Darwin was horrified. The *Beagle* looked like a wreck! The masts were damaged, the deck was full of holes, and the hull was leaking badly. No-one could sail in a ship like that!

Originally, HMS *Beagle* was built as a brig (right). This was a common type of Navy warship, used for coastal voyages. It had two masts, carrying square-rigged sails at right-angles to the mast. The lower part of the main mast was fitted with a an extra "fore and aft" sail, carried parallel to the deck.

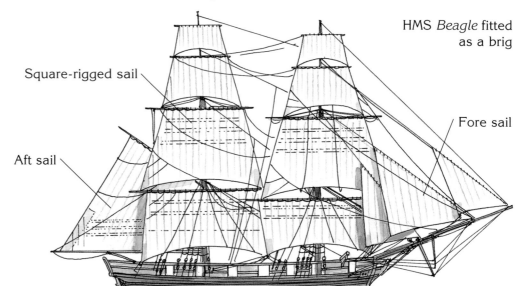

HMS *Beagle* fitted as a brig

Square-rigged sail

Aft sail

Fore sail

HMS *Beagle* fitted as a barque

Mizzen mast

In 1825, HMS *Beagle* was changed to make her more suitable for survey work in distant seas and oceans. She was converted into a barque (another popular Navy ship design, left). A third mast (called a mizzenmast) was added towards the stern (rear) of the ship. She carried fore-and-aft sails.

The new mast and sails made the *Beagle* faster and easier to steer. This was important in uncharted waters, where there might be shallows or hidden rocks around coasts or close to coral reefs. Surveyors like Darwin and Fitzroy needed a ship they could quickly steer away from danger.

By October 1831, the *Beagle* was repaired and watertight. She was ready to set sail to South America, then round the world. Her decks were scrubbed, and her masts and stays (ropes supporting them) were coated in pitch as a preservative. Her bilges (bottom of the hold) had been pumped clean of water.

READY TO SAIL

In Plymouth Fitzroy did his best to calm Darwin's fears. He promised Darwin that the *Beagle* would soon be seaworthy and ready to sail. Darwin went to Cambridge to ask his old tutor, Professor Henslow, to look after any specimens of wildlife he might send home from distant lands. Next he went to Shropshire to say farewell to his family. After this he travelled to London to buy more supplies for the voyage. He also visited museums to seek information and advice from experts. He wanted to find out all he could about plants, animals and rocks. He also practiced taxidermy—preserving dead animals by curing, and then stuffing their skins to retain their lifelike appearance

Meanwhile, back in Plymouth, repair work on HMS *Beagle* was taking longer than expected. Darwin did not mind. It gave him more time to consult experts in London. But at last the ship was ready. Loaded with scientific equipment, Darwin set out to join the *Beagle* voyage.

Darwin came on board the *Beagle* with many different devices, all designed to record everything, including creatures, that he hoped to observe on the voyage. His equipment included:
A microscope
A geological compass
A geological hammer (to chip specimens off rocks)
An ordinary compass
A telescope
A barometer (to measure air pressure and forecast weather)
A clinometer (to measure slopes of mountains)
A hygrometer (to measure the density of liquids)

CAPTAIN AND CREW

For two months—October and November 1831—Darwin and the *Beagle* crew waited in Plymouth. Their ship was ready, but the weather was too bad to let them set sail. The *Beagle* tried to leave harbor on November 15, but was driven back by strong westerly gales. Darwin wrote in his dairy that this time was "the most miserable I ever spent." He began to feel ill, with chest pains and flutterings in his heart. Possibly this illness was worsened by stress. Finally the weather improved, and the *Beagle* left Plymouth on December 27, 1831. As soon as the ship reached open water Darwin felt terribly seasick. He suffered from this malady for the whole of the five-year voyage.

Besides Darwin and the *Beagle*'s captain, Fitzroy, there were 72 people on board. Darwin was treated with respect, as if he were an officer. He had his own cabin and ate his meals at the captain's table. Unlike other crew members, he received no pay. Instead his family paid around £500 (approximately $900,000 today) to cover the cost of his food and lodging during the voyage. Also, unlike the crew, who were under the captain's command, Darwin was independent—he had permission to leave the ship whenever he wanted to.

Artist   Mate   Fitzroy   Marine captain   Lieutenant   Darwin   Sergeant   Sailor

Like other British Navy ships, the *Beagle* carried marines (onboard soldiers). Their task was to defend the ship and deal with violent crime or mutinies on board.

Marines were armed with muskets (long guns fired with gunpowder that shot small lead balls) and pistols (small, powerful hand-held guns). Their officers carried swords.

Three of the four Native South Americans brought to England by Captain Fitzroy were passengers on the voyage. One died in England before the *Beagle* sailed.

On board were men with essential skills like a sail-maker and the ship's doctor. There was also an artist to record landscapes and wildlife on the voyage.

Thirty-four crew members kept the ship sailing. They raised and lowered sails, climbed the rigging, cleaned the decks, kept lookout, and cooked food.

The captain and three officers gave orders to the crew, plotted the ship's course, and planned the voyage. Darwin and his servant, Symes Covington, were civilians.

As well as adult men the crew contained eight boys, who were trainee sailors. They ran errands, helped the adults, and tried to learn from all that happened on board.

Like other British Navy captains, Fiztroy used violence to make the crew obey him. Darwin hated hearing groans from those sailors being whipped as punishment.

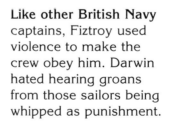

Master

Boatswain

Spare wood

Gun powder

Water and meat

Sets of sails

Guns

Stores

LIFE ON BOARD

On its historic voyage round the world, HMS *Beagle* spent four years, nine months and five days at sea. For all of that time, Darwin's home on board was a tiny cabin, eleven feet long and nine feet wide. The walls were lined with bookshelves. There was a small oven (for heat), a wash-stand, a chest of drawers, an instrument cabinet, a water closet and a large chart table. The mizzen-mast passed right through the cabin, from floor to ceiling. All this left just a tiny space for Darwin to work in. Darwin shared the captain's table for meals, except when they quarrelled. Darwin's seasickness, chest pains and palpitations (fluttering heart) often kept him confined to his bed—a hammock slung above the chart table!

Like everyone else on board, Darwin's life was ruled by the ship's daily routine. The crew took turns to work in watches of four hours work and four hours rest, throughout the day and night. Loud bells at the end of each watch woke up almost everyone on board. The wind in the sails and the rigging, shouts from officers and men, feet pounding on the deck, and occasional outbreaks of drunkenness among the crew all made the ship a very noisy place to be. As captain, Fitzroy was responsible for maintaining discipline on board. He was famous for his hot temper—Darwin called him "unreasonable"—and punished his sailors with floggings if they disobeyed orders or failed to carry out their daily tasks.

According to British sailors' tradition, anyone on board ship who crossed the equator for the first time was either thrown overboard on a rope, or had to pay a fine (usually a large amount of rum or beer). This was said to be an offering to Neptune, the Roman god of the sea.

EVERYDAY LIFE ON BOARD SHIP

Survey vessels (small ships for shallow waters) set sail.

Repairing canvas sails torn by high winds or rotted by salty sea water.

Taking exercise and fresh air on deck when recovering from sea-sickness.

Captain hears reports from officers of bad behavior by crew members.

Officers use a sextant to measure the position of the sun and stars to find the ship's position.

Sailors take soundings – measuring the depth of sea using a long rope with a weight at the end.

Captain records the course (track) sailed by the ship, and consults charts (ocean maps).

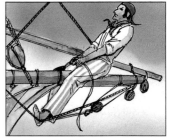

Crew use the huge capstan to wind the heavy ropes used for mooring and anchoring.

Crew sling hammocks – used for sleeping—in any free space they can find below deck.

Time on board ship is measured by a chronometer, and sounded by ringing bells.

Sailors climb the rigging to check and repair it, and to untangle knotted ropes.

Sailors balance on yards (beams) high above the deck to reef (shorten) sails.

To keep the ship clean sailors scrub the decks with seawater every day.

The ship's guns need cleaning each time they are fired, and polishing in peacetime.

Officers eat at the captain's table; the crew eat on deck or sheltered below.

The helmsman steers the ship with the wheel, following the captain's orders.

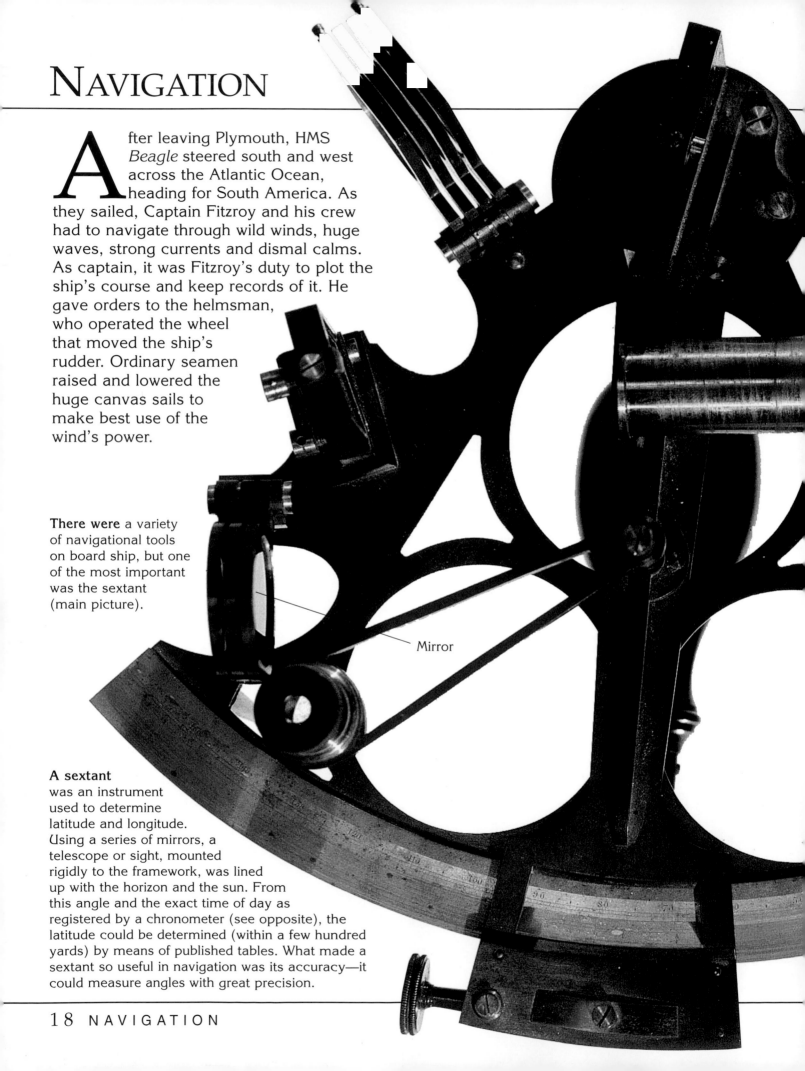

NAVIGATION

After leaving Plymouth, HMS *Beagle* steered south and west across the Atlantic Ocean, heading for South America. As they sailed, Captain Fitzroy and his crew had to navigate through wild winds, huge waves, strong currents and dismal calms. As captain, it was Fitzroy's duty to plot the ship's course and keep records of it. He gave orders to the helmsman, who operated the wheel that moved the ship's rudder. Ordinary seamen raised and lowered the huge canvas sails to make best use of the wind's power.

There were a variety of navigational tools on board ship, but one of the most important was the sextant (main picture).

Mirror

A sextant was an instrument used to determine latitude and longitude. Using a series of mirrors, a telescope or sight, mounted rigidly to the framework, was lined up with the horizon and the sun. From this angle and the exact time of day as registered by a chronometer (see opposite), the latitude could be determined (within a few hundred yards) by means of published tables. What made a sextant so useful in navigation was its accuracy—it could measure angles with great precision.

On January 6, 1832 the *Beagle* reached the Canary Islands off West Africa. But no one on board went ashore for fear of catching cholera. The *Beagle* sailed on, reaching the Cape Verde Islands on January 16, then crossing the equator to arrive in Brazil on February 28.

At Cape Verde, Darwin made observations of sea-creatures, especially cuttlefish. He tried to work out how they changed color, and why. He also noticed bands of sea-shells in cliffs high above the sea. They had obviously once been under water. How and when had they risen?

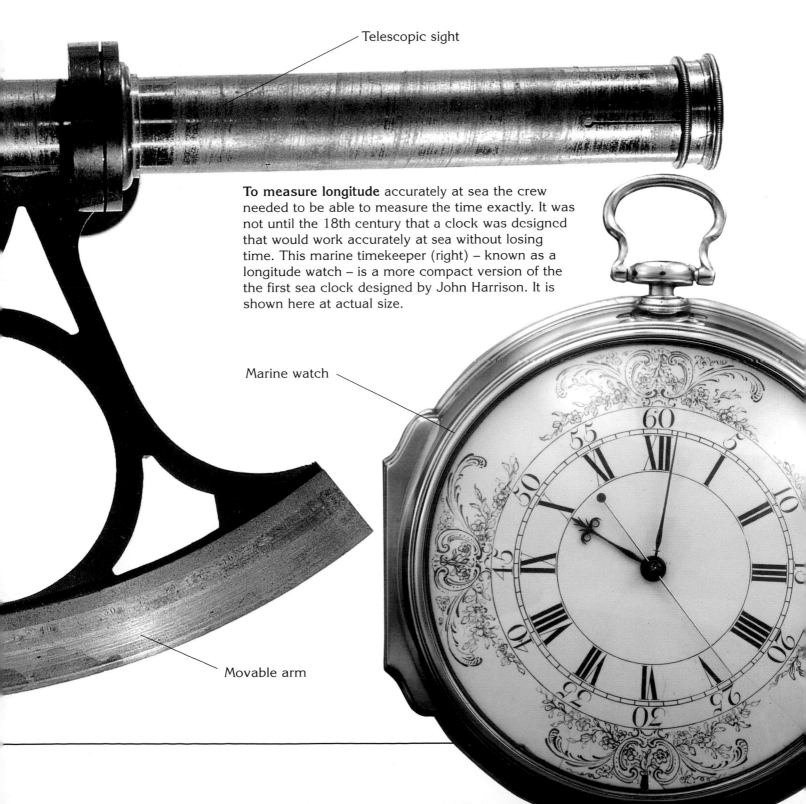

Telescopic sight

To measure longitude accurately at sea the crew needed to be able to measure the time exactly. It was not until the 18th century that a clock was designed that would work accurately at sea without losing time. This marine timekeeper (right) – known as a longitude watch – is a more compact version of the the first sea clock designed by John Harrison. It is shown here at actual size.

Marine watch

Movable arm

EXPLORING THE RAINFOREST

The *Beagle* ended its Atlantic crossing and anchored off the port of Salvador, Brazil on February 28, 1832. After a short stay she sailed south. Darwin had been suffering from seasickness, so he stayed on dry land while Fitzroy and his crew explored shallow seas along the Brazilian coast. While they were away, Darwin seized the chance to go exploring in the rainforest. In 18 days he travelled over 149 miles on foot and horseback, then rented a cottage to use as a base for writing up his expedition notes and making scientific experiments. Darwin was amazed and excited by all the strange wildlife he observed. He eagerly recorded the size, shape and behavior of all kinds of creatures, including monkeys, jaguars, vampire bats, frogs with suckers on their feet, spiders, fireflies, jumping beetles and "talking" butterflies, that seemed to communicate with each other in a series of clicks. He was fascinated by massive tree-trunks covered in parasitic plants, and had to hack his way along paths blocked by rainforest creepers. He recorded amazingly heavy rainfall, and disgustingly smelly fungi. Looking back at this time, he commented, "It was impossible to wish for anything more delightful."

In April, May and June 1832, Fitzroy steered the *Beagle* along the coast of South America, from Salvador to Rio de Janiero. Then he sailed further south to Montevideo (now in Uruguay). Everywhere the *Beagle* went Fitzroy made surveys, and mapped the shore. On visits to Brazilian ports his crew purchased supplies for the next stage of the voyage.

As the *Beagle* sailed, her crew took soundings to measure the depth of the sea by lowering a weighted rope, marked in fathoms.

They collected samples of sand, mud and gravel from the sea-bed by dragging a wax-filled tube along the bottom.

While the *Beagle* was at sea Darwin stayed on shore. He rented a cottage near Mount Corcovado, inland from Rio.

He collected specimens, preserved them in spirit (alcohol), made notes, and sent letters home. Augustus Earle, the ship's artist, stayed with him.

Darwin was shocked and disgusted by the treatment of slaves in Brazil.

Darwin observed how monkeys used their prehensile tails to grip hold of trees.

On the rainforest floor Darwin saw ants' nests nearly 13 feet high.

Darwin collected nine species of snakes and eighty different kinds of birds.

Hummingbirds fluttered so quickly that Darwin said they looked like moths.

The *Beagle*'s surgeon was jealous of Darwin's work, and sailed home.

FINDING FOSSILS

In July, with Darwin on board, the *Beagle* set sail again, bound for Montevideo (now in Uruguay). From there Darwin sent his first load of wildlife specimens to his old professor at Cambridge University. It included plants, rocks, beetles, sea-creatures, and whole animals preserved in alcohol.

Late in August 1832 the *Beagle* sailed south again to Bahia Blanca in Argentina, before heading out to sea to make more surveys. Darwin stayed behind to make new expeditions on shore. This time he planned to make a collection of fossils. He had briefly studied geology (the science of the earth) back home in England. Now he had the opportunity to find out more. Some of the world's greatest fossil-beds were close by. Below layers of rock in cliffs at Puenta Arena (now in Patagonia) Darwin found gigantic fossil bones and teeth that must have belonged to enormous, amazing animals. But what were they, and how did they live? Darwin was puzzled. He could not identify the fossils, and no other scientist had ever reported such finds.

As the *Beagle* sailed south from Rio de Janeiro, hundreds of porpoises (above) came alongside, swimming very fast and leaping out of the water. Darwin called it an "extraordinary spectacle." These South Atlantic dolphins had not been described by scientists before. Darwin later named them after Captain Fitzroy.

Montevideo was a busy port run by settlers from Spain. They owned large numbers of African slaves, and traded with European ranchers and miners from further inland. On July 31, 1832 the Montevideo police chief asked Captain Fitzroy to help put down a rebellion. Fitzroy sent 50 armed men.

Many on board the *Beagle* were horrified by Darwin's collections of smelly, slimy sea creatures and huge, dusty fossils. They complained that this "useless junk" made too much mess.

Slowly Darwin began to understand what he was seeing. The fossils he had found did not belong to species that had become extinct long ago. Instead they were the remains of creatures related to animals still living in South America, such as sloths and armadillos. As soon as he could—in November 1832—Darwin sent specimens back to England. If he had identified the fossils correctly, his findings were going to challenge some very important ideas!

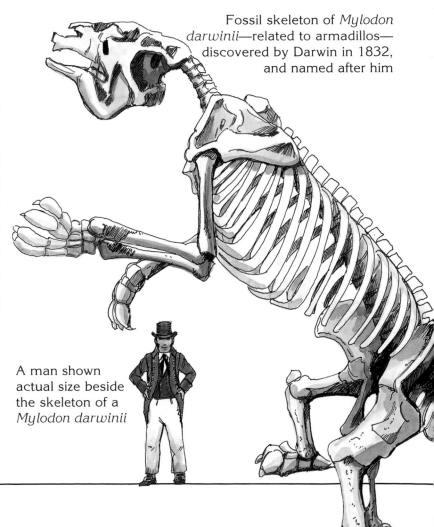

Fossil skeleton of *Mylodon darwinii*—related to armadillos—discovered by Darwin in 1832, and named after him

Like many people of his time, Captain Fitzroy believed that life on earth had been destroyed by the great Flood told of in the Bible, then re-created by God. Darwin disagreed. From the layers of rock in which he found his fossils, he knew they must be millions of years old. But their descendants were still living! So life on earth could not have been destroyed.

A man shown actual size beside the skeleton of a *Mylodon darwinii*

LAND OF ICE AND FIRE

Again the *Beagle* sailed south. It was heading for Tierra del Fuego—islands at the tip of South America. Named "Land of Fire" in Spanish, its rugged mountains were always capped with ice, and snow fell even in summertime. This harsh environment was home to three passengers on the *Beagle*—young native people captured by Captain Fitzroy on his earlier South American voyage. A devout Christian, Fitzroy hoped they would spread the Christian faith among the islanders and teach them to give up their old simple ways of living. The *Beagle* arrived off Tierra del Fuego in December 1832, but the weather was so bad that it could not sail close to the shore. At last, on January 18, 1833, the crew and passengers landed. Darwin was fascinated to see the local people, and impressed by their survival skills. But he was also amazed by the contrast between their lifestyle and his own. He wrote that he could hardly believe that they, and he, were "inhabitants of the same world."

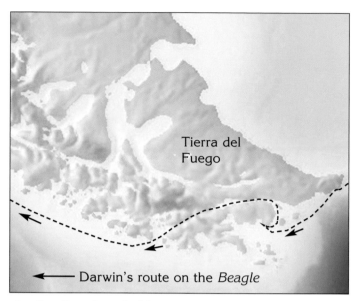

Tierra del Fuego

◄—— Darwin's route on the *Beagle*

As the *Beagle* sailed between the islands of Tierra del Fuego, crowds of Native peoples rushed shouting and waving along the shore. They lit beacon fires on cliffs and hills to warn other islanders of the approaching ship.

HMS *Beagle* sailing past the towering mountains of Tierra del Fuego.

In 1826 Fitzroy captured four native people. But one died soon after reaching England. He gave them new names.

Jemmy Button was about 14 years old. He was plump, friendly and cheerful.

Fuegia Basket was only 9 years old. She was pretty, shy and quick to learn languages.

York Minister was about 26 years old. He was quiet, clever, and very strong.

Fitzroy paid for the three surviving native people to be cared for in England. They were given fine clothes, learned English, and were taught polite manners.

Fitzroy also arranged for these three native people to learn about the Christian faith. He hoped to help spread his faith all around the world.

In January 1833 the *Beagle* arrived at Tierra del Fuego, and Jemmy, Fuegia and York were taken ashore. The Reverend Richard Matthews, a missionary, went with them.

Local people helped Matthews unload stocks of food, seeds, tools and clothes, build three large shelters, and dig two plots for growing vegetables.

This drawing was published in 1839 in Captain Fitzroy's book about the *Beagle* voyage. It shows a native man from Tierra del Fuego.

COWBOYS AND MISSIONARIES

For a short while, the *Beagle* rested at sea, while Darwin explored cliffs and glaciers. On February 6, 1833, she sailed back to the shelters that had been built for Jemmy, Fuegia, and York and found that they had been destroyed. Reverend Matthews, the missionary, decided that his task was hopeless and rejoined the *Beagle*. But Jemmy, Fuegia and York all decided to stay. They rebuilt the shelters and replanted the gardens, and the *Beagle* sailed away.

South America

ATLANTIC OCEAN

PACIFIC OCEAN

From February 1832 to April 1934 Fitzroy surveyed the east coast of South America in the *Beagle*. From April 1834 to October 1835 he surveyed the west coast.

Darwin watched gauchos throwing "bolas"—heavy balls on ropes—to catch wild creatures for food. But when he tried throwing one himself, he snared his own horse and got tangled in some bushes.

As the *Beagle* was moored up in the Falkland Islands Darwin collected fossils. He noticed that they were different from other South American ones. He decided that from now on he should take samples from everywhere he visited, so that he could make careful scientific comparisons. Later these comparisons helped Darwin work out important new theories about how and why living creatures adapted to their own environment. On April 6, 1833, the *Beagle* left the Falklands and returned to Montevideo on South America's east coast. Darwin disliked the city and went exploring inland, where he collected many examples of plants and animals and met local cowboys, called Gauchos.

The *Beagle* sailed among the islands of Tierra del Fuego. The mountainous scenery in the Ponsonby Sound (below) was magnificent, and Darwin was able to observe how ice broke off mountain glaciers and crashed into the sea.

From May to November 1833, Darwin spent most of his time ashore. He went riding with the Gauchos, and enjoyed eating, drinking and singing around their camp fires. He learned about local wildlife, such as guanacos (wild llama), agoutis (giant rats) and incredibly smelly deer. He sent letters home and received permission from his father to hire a servant to help with his scientific work. He also sent many more specimens back to scientists in Cambridge. Most exciting of all, Darwin found yet more fossils. These were far inland, but buried under a layer of fossilized sea-shells. One fossil puzzled him tremendously, because it was not like living local species. Had this creature lived in a sea that had disappeared long ago? And had this creature died out with no descendants because the environment had changed?

EARTHQUAKE AND LAND RISING

At last Darwin rejoined the *Beagle* and set sail, reaching Tierra del Fuego in March 1834. But a shock lay in wait—the missionary huts were in ruins! Jemmy Button appeared and greeted Fitzroy. He explained that he had been attacked and that York and Fuegia had run away. Next the *Beagle* sailed north to survey the Santa Cruz valley in Patagonia, where Darwin observed more fossil shells in cliffs high above waterlevel. After calling again at the Falklands, the *Beagle* rounded South America. On June 11, 1834, she sailed into the Pacific Ocean and headed northwards along the coast of Chile. As usual Darwin tried to arrange scientific expeditions on shore. But he fell ill and had to rest until the end of 1834. In January 1835, he witnessed a dramatic eruption. The next month he survived a massive earthquake, which devastated the Chilean coastal city of Concepcion.

After the earthquake a huge tidal wave rushed inland, carrying whole ships with it. Darwin also saw how the earthquake had forced some land upwards, so it was much higher than before. This provided evidence for his theory that land could rise, sea-levels could fall, and environments could change completely.

Darwin and his team climbing in the Andes

To explain the fossil shells high up in the cliffs, Darwin put forward a new theory: the land of South America must be rising, and sea levels falling.

Fossil sea-shells found in the Andes

Various species of beetle

Everywhere he went Darwin tried to collect samples of local wildlife. In Chile he watched natives using traditional methods to capture the majestic condor, either tempting them with carrion or noosing them in low tree branches.

Darwin and Fitzroy watched molten lava shoot from erupting Mount Osorno—a "very magnificent spectacle."

The crew of the *Beagle* visiting the city of Concepcion, devastated during the earthquake.

TURTLE ISLANDS

Darwin stayed in Chile until July 1835. He collected specimens from the high Andes mountains and studied the effects of the great earthquake. Then he sailed north to Lima in Peru. There the *Beagle's* crew prepared for a long voyage out into the Pacific Ocean.

On September 7, the *Beagle* set sail for the Galapagos—a group of volcanic islands almost 621 miles off the coast of Ecuador. Straight away Darwin wanted to investigate their strange black lava rocks and varied environments. He collected plants, small animals, rock samples and insects. He saw that most of the wildlife was related to other South American species, but that it was not exactly the same.

Next Darwin examined the giant tortoises on the islands. Why were they so much bigger than anywhere else in the world? Local people told Darwin that the tortoises were different on each separate island. Later, back home in England, he used this observation to help create an important new theory about the whole natural world.

1. Geospiza magnirostris.
2. Geospiza fortis.
3. Geospiza parvula.
4. Certhidea olivacea.

Darwin counted 13 different types of finch living on the Galapagos. All were found only on the islands, and nowhere else in the world. They were all closely related, but their heads—and especially their beaks—were not all the same. Darwin concluded that finches on each island had adapted their beaks to eat the different food-plants growing in each habitat. But, as yet, he could not work out precisely how this had happened.

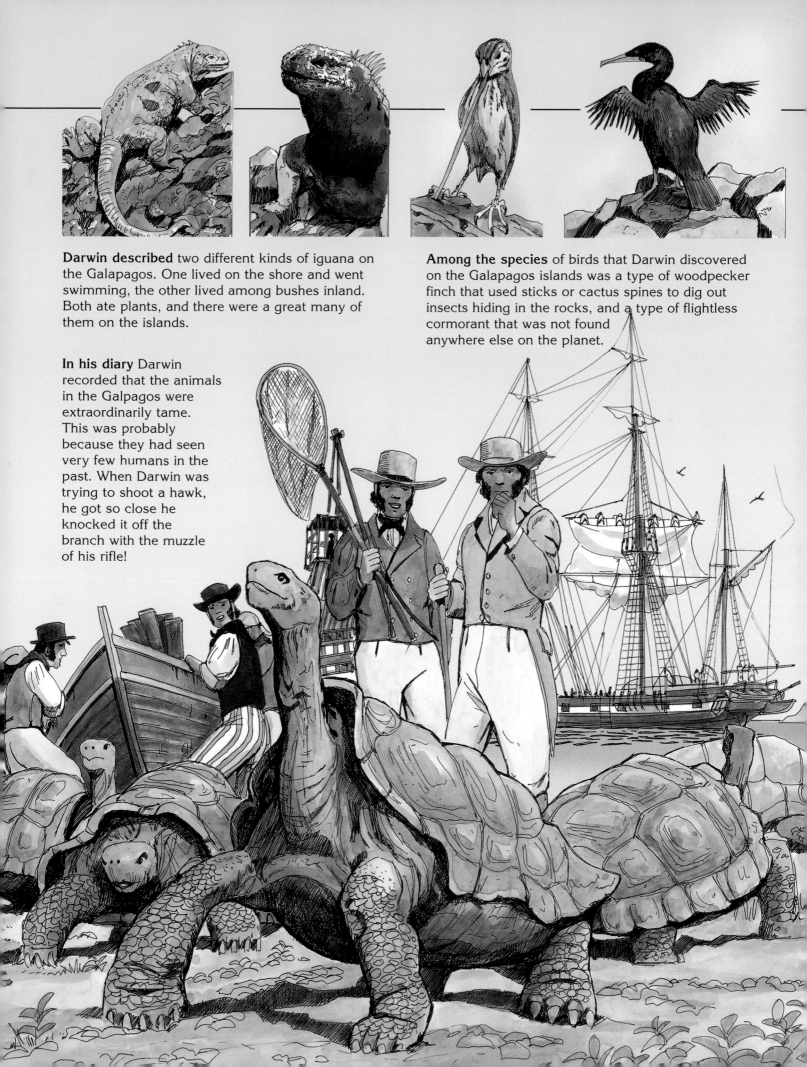

Darwin described two different kinds of iguana on the Galapagos. One lived on the shore and went swimming, the other lived among bushes inland. Both ate plants, and there were a great many of them on the islands.

In his diary Darwin recorded that the animals in the Galpagos were extraordinarily tame. This was probably because they had seen very few humans in the past. When Darwin was trying to shoot a hawk, he got so close he knocked it off the branch with the muzzle of his rifle!

Among the species of birds that Darwin discovered on the Galapagos islands was a type of woodpecker finch that used sticks or cactus spines to dig out insects hiding in the rocks, and a type of flightless cormorant that was not found anywhere else on the planet.

ISLAND QUEEN

The *Beagle* sailed from the Galapagos on October 20, 1835, and headed west across the Pacific. Thanks to strong winds and steady seas it reached the island of Tahiti, 3,106 miles away, just 26 days later. As the *Beagle* approached the island, Darwin marvelled at the coral reef that surrounded it. Once ashore Darwin recruited guides to help him explore. He examined the flora that grew on the lower slopes of the mountains and the abundance of wild food plants, such as breadfruit and bananas. Like earlier visitors to Tahiti, he found the island beautiful and the people friendly, intelligent and good-looking. He commented that the plentiful food supply made the islanders strong and handsome, and wrote that it would not take long before "a dark skin" became "more pleasing and natural to the eye of a European than this own color." He compared white skin to a plant that had been artificially bleached by growing in unusual conditions. These observations were made over 100 years before other scientists began to think that human beings might have originated in Africa, with dark skins.

In November Fitzroy and Darwin invited Queen Pomarre of Tahiti on board the *Beagle* (right). They sent four boats to fetch her, each decorated with flags. Captain Fitzroy offered the queen presents, which she graciously accepted. Then he used some of the *Beagle*'s distress rockets to stage a firework display. After this, the *Beagle* sailors sang; the Queen enjoyed their performance, especially the noisy songs.

On November 17, Darwin recorded that before breakfast the *Beagle* was surrounded by a fleet of canoes. They carried around 200 Tahitians, who came to trade with the sailors. The Tahitians offered beautiful tropical shells for sale. Darwin was impressed by their honest, peaceful behavior.

NEW ZEALAND AND AUSTRALIA

The *Beagle* arrived off New Zealand on December 19, 1835. Darwin found the island rather disappointing. He was shocked by the poor and dirty living conditions of many Maori people and by their traditional passion for fighting. He tried to study the native New Zealand wildlife, but found it very difficult to travel far inland. Away from European and Maori settlements the land was overgrown with giant ferns and small bushes, which were almost impossible to walk through.

In Australia Darwin observed native Australian animals, such as kangaroos and duck-billed platypus, and native trees, such as eucalyptus. He admired the way the Aboriginal people had adapted their way of life to the Australian environment, but feared for their future. He predicted that it would soon be destroyed by European settlers, and that the Maori communities in New Zealand would be wiped out in the same way. He commented that, just like animals, stronger groups of humans always destroy weaker ones. Later in life Darwin would use this idea to help explain how all living creatures changed over time.

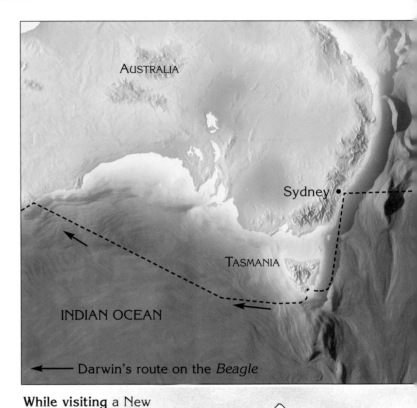

Darwin's route on the *Beagle*

While visiting a New Zealand village Darwin watched Maori people rubbing noses—a traditional friendly greeting. Using a scientific approach to behavior, he compared this to an English handshake, but said it lasted longer.

Darwin admired Maori men's courage and energy, but he believed that traditional Maori tattoos weakened their face muscles, and gave them an unpleasantly stern, rigid expression.

New Zealand

South Pacific Ocean

Head of a Maori

Head of an Australian Aborigine

Darwin was impressed by Aboriginal hunters. He greatly admired their tracking and spear-throwing skills, and their ability to disguise and conceal themselves to trap their prey.

In February 1836 Darwin watched traditional Aboriginal dances (below). He described groups of men, painted with white lines, running and stamping, and dances where they imitated emus or kangaroos. He reported that everyone was in high spirits and that Aboriginal women and children enjoyed the dancing. He thought that the dances represented hunting or wars.

On Mauritius, Captain Lloyd, the Surveyor-General, arranged for Darwin to have a ride on his elephant—the only one on Mauritius. Darwin was surprised at how silently the elephant walked along.

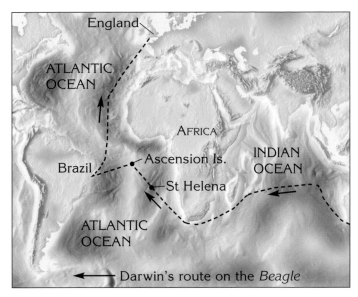

After leaving Mauritius the *Beagle* rounded the southern tip of Africa, and then sailed west to St. Helena, Ascension Island and Brazil. Fitzroy wanted to check time measurements that he had made earlier in the voyage. After calling briefly at the Azores Islands in August 1836, the *Beagle* sailed for home.

In March 1836 the *Beagle* left Australia, and headed west. In April she called at the Cocos Islands, where Darwin observed how the local land-crabs had huge front claws that helped them open coconuts—the only available food. Sailing on, the *Beagle* reached the island of Mauritius on April 29. They were welcomed by local officials, who took them on a tour. Darwin also spent time with Fitzroy, who was surveying the shallow waters of the coral reef that surrounded Mauritius. He wondered how, and why, the corals grew there. What were they resting on? How did they form such well-organized "walls"? Darwin also observed that corals on the inside of the reef had died, because the still, shallow waters there did not suit them. Why do some creatures "sacrifice" their lives for the good of their community or for their species as a whole? Even today scientists do not all agree on the answer to that question.

On their way home the crew stopped in Brazil. Darwin was only too happy to leave, however, because he loathed the practice of slavery, which still took place there. He later wrote in his journal: "I thank God, I shall never again visit a slave-country."

The *Beagle* reached England after a voyage which lasted almost five years. It was night-time and raining when Fitzroy docked his ship in the south-western port of Falmouth, after battling though a heavy storm.

Darwin left the *Beagle* and set off for his parents' home. His voyage had taught him so much and given him many new ideas.

HOW, WHY, WHEN?

Back home in England Darwin tried to make sense of all the new knowledge he had gained. He wrote scientific reports and edited his travel diary for publication. He read new works by other scientists, such as Thomas Malthus, an expert on human population. Slowly he became convinced that life on earth had not been created—either before or after the Flood—in the state that he had seen it in. He felt certain that all living creatures must have changed and developed over time. But how, why and when had this happened? Malthus's ideas about human populations gave Darwin a clue.

Malthus argued that humans and all other creatures have the ability to produce more offspring than can possibly survive. Among humans, population size is limited by the amount of food available. If food runs short the weakest people die. Darwin realized that this harsh fact of life might also be the reason why plants and animals changed. Only the ones best suited to their environment would survive. A bird might pass a useful characteristic, such as a longer beak, on to its descendants. Slowly, over the centuries, this would change the way a whole group of animals looked or behaved. Darwin called this process "Natural Selection."

In his journal Darwin looked back at the long years he had spent on the *Beagle* voyage. He had missed his family and friends. His girlfriend had married another man. He had lived in cramped quarters, eaten stale food and been terribly sick. Although his scientific work kept him occupied, at times the vast ocean had seemed boring. But, Darwin decided, all these troubles and dangers had been worthwhile, because they had produced a "harvest" of knowledge.

Darwin realized that Natural Selection could explain many of the things that had puzzled him on his travels. It was why the Galapagos finches were different from island to island. It was why rainforest orchids had such beautiful flowers—to attract insects to spread pollen to fertilize them. It was why some beetles were the same color as the vegetation they lived on—the camouflage protected them. It was even why fossils were different from their living relatives—they had died out because they were the weaker forms of their species! Developing his theory, Darwin also realized that Natural Selection might explain why embryos from different species often looked the same. (You can read more about this on pages 40 and 41.)

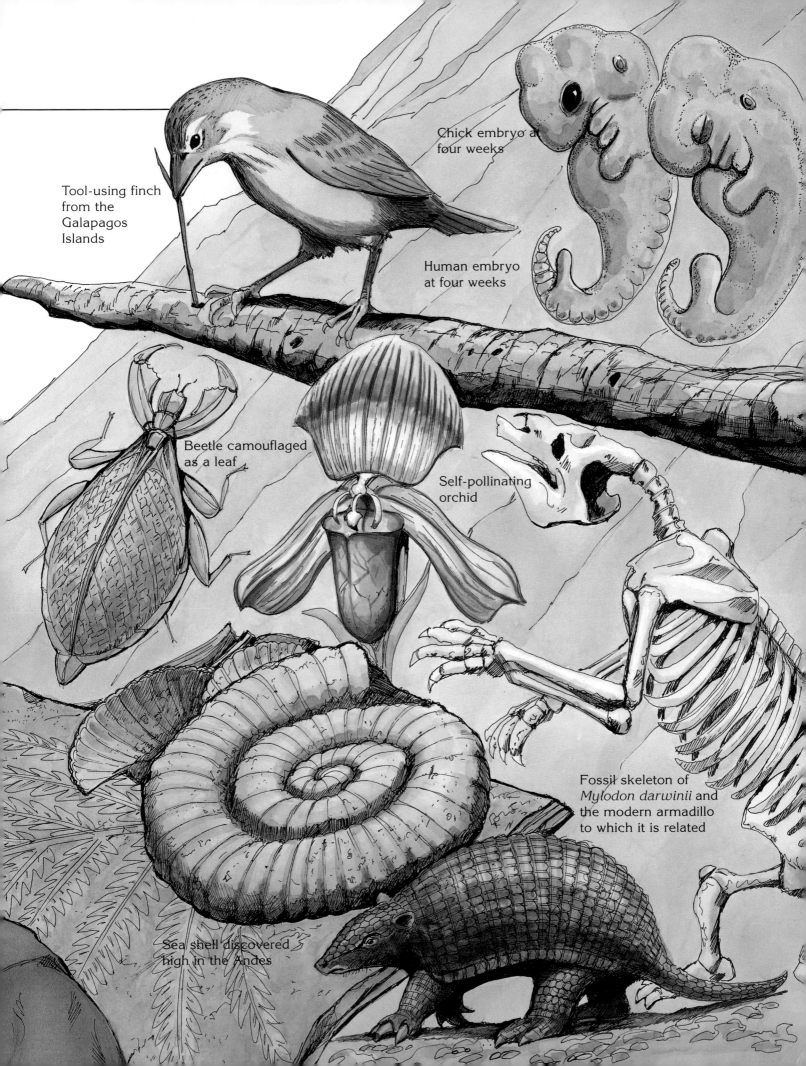

Tool-using finch from the Galapagos Islands

Chick embryo at four weeks

Human embryo at four weeks

Beetle camouflaged as a leaf

Self-pollinating orchid

Fossil skeleton of *Mylodon darwinii* and the modern armadillo to which it is related

Sea shell discovered high in the Andes

APES AND HUMANS

arwin knew that his theory of Natural Selection would be very controversial. It particularly upset Christian people (including Darwin's own family), because it challenged the Bible's descriptions of how the earth was created. At first Darwin did not discuss human development in his writings. But he believed that humans changed over time to survive in their environment, just like any other animal. His work on animal embryos also led him to think that the descendants of one ancestor might slowly develop in different ways. In 1871 he made his revolutionary suggestion: apes and humans were descended from the same ancestor.

In 1839 Darwin married his first cousin, Emma Wedgwood. They had 10 children, three of whom died young. They lived in a large house in the english countryside (Downe House, Kent), surrounded by fields and gardens, where Darwin could work in peace. Darwin also needed time to rest and recover from attacks of a mysterious illness that plagued him for the rest of his life. Some historians think this was Chagas Disease—an infection carried by blood-sucking insects that live in South America. Darwin certainly reported being bitten by these. But other historians think that his illness was caused by stress, anxiety and shyness.

In *The Descent of Man* (published in 1871), Darwin suggested that humans had changed over time and that they shared an ancestor with apes, who had developed differently.

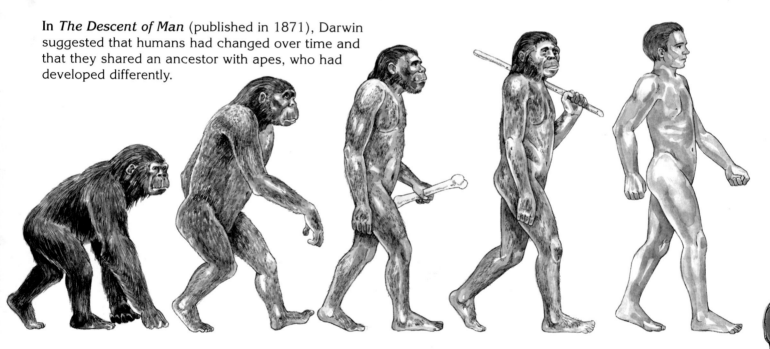

Darwin's study of geology led him to suggest that the earth had not been created by God. He was the first to explain how coral (which only grows in shallow water) created reefs deep under the sea.

As coral attaches to the edges of an island it forms a ring around the outside. This is called a "fringing reef."

If the sea rises the island shrinks away under the water, but the coral remains. This is called a "barrier reef."

If the island becomes completely submerged, only the coral remains in a large ring. This is called an "atoll."

Darwin sometimes let his children help with research. He studied plants and insects in the family's garden, and explained how earthworms improve garden soil.

EVOLUTION

arwin spent many years at home, reading, thinking and studying, before writing a book to explain his theory of Natural Selection to the world. He probably only finished it because he heard that another younger scientist, Alfred Wallace, was beginning to develop similar ideas. But, when Darwin's book was at last published in 1859, all copies were sold on the very first day.

Soon Darwin's theory of Natural Selection became the basis of another very important idea known as Evolution. This is the suggestion (believed by most scientists today) that all animal and plant species can be traced back to a single common ancestor: the first living thing on earth. Over millions of years, through Natural Selection, each species has changed and developed countless differences. Most scientists think that "evolutionary" change is still going on today.

This magazine illustration from 1891 is a humorous drawing showing the ascent of man from ape, suggesting that perhaps we have not evolved as far as we think. It shows that Darwin's discoveries had become well-known by the late nineteenth century.

Darwin was not the first scientist to suggest that animals changed and developed over time. But he was the first to suggest how this might happen, through Natural Selection. He was also the first to be able to support this theory with an enormous amount of "real life" comparative evidence, gathered all round the world on his *Beagle* voyage.

Darwin never argued about his new theories in public—he was too shy. But in 1860, one of his keenest supporters, Thomas Henry Huxley, staged a debate with the Bishop of Oxford, who held the Christian view that God had created everything on earth. Huxley won. Darwin's old acquaintance, Fitzroy, who was captain of the *Beagle*, also took part in the debate, but on the Bishop's side.

Darwin's book explaining his theory was called *On the Origin of Species by Means of Natural Selection*. Even today it remains one of the most important scientific works ever written.

People found Darwin's ideas so shocking that they made jokes about them. They were most alarmed by the thought that humans were descended from monkeys, even though Darwin never made that claim. (He said that they shared the same distant ancestor.)

Timeline of the Voyage

1831

December 27: Set sail from Plymouth

1832

January 18-February 8: Cape Verde Islands
February 28-March 18: Bahia
April 4-July 5: Rio de Janeiro
April 8-23: Excursions to various estates inland
July 26-August 19: Montevideo
September 6-October 17: Bahia Blanca
November 2-26: Montevideo
December 16-February 26, 1833: Tierra del Fuego

1833

March1-April 6: Falkland Islands
April 28-July 23: Maldonado
August 3-24: Mouth of the Rio Negro
August11-17: Excursion from El Carmen to Bahia Blanca
August 24-October 6: Surveying the Argentinian Coast
September 8-20: Excursion from Bahia Blanca to Buenos Aires
October 6-19: Maldonado
September 27-October 20: Excursion to Santa Fe and along the Parana
October 21-December 6: Montevideo
November 14-28: Excursion to Mercedes 1834
December 23-January 4, 1834: Port Desire

1834

January 9-19: Port St Julian
January 29-March 7: Tierra del Fuego
March 10-April 7: Falkland Islands
April 13-May12: Santa Cruz river
April 18-May 8: Excursion up the Santa Cruz river

June 28-July13: Chiloe
July 31-November 10: Valparaiso
August14-September 27: Excursion into the Andes
November 21-February 4, 1835: Chileo and Chronos archipelago

1835

February 8-22: Valdivia
March 4-7: Concepcion
March 11-17: Valparaiso
March 13-April 10: Excursion from Santiago, across the Andes to Mendoza
March 27-April 17: Neighborhood of Concepcion
17th April to 27th June: Chilean coast
April 27-July 4: Excursion to Coquimbo and Copiapo
July 12-15: Iquiqui (Peru)
July 19-September 7: Callao
September 16-October 20: Galapagos Islands
November 15-26: Tahiti
December 21-30: New Zealand

1836

January 12-30: Sydney
February 2-17: Hobart, Tasmania
March 3-14: King George's Sound
April 2-12: Cocos (Keeling) Islands
April 29-May 9: Mauritius
May 31-June18: Cape of Good Hope
July 7-14: St Helena
July 19-23: Ascencion Island
August 1-6: Bahia
August 12-17: Pernabucco
October 2: Charles Darwin arrives at Falmouth, Cornwall, England.

DARWIN'S LIFE AND WORKS

1809	Born February 12 in Shropshire, England
1817	Darwin's mother, Susannah, died when he was just eight years old
1818-1825	Attended grammar school in Shrewsbury but was taken out by his father for getting poor grades
1825-1827	Darwin spent the summer of 1825 working in his father's medical practice before being sent to Edinburgh University to train for a medical career
1827	Darwin quit medical school and went to Cambridge University to study for the clergy
1831	Graduated from Cambridge University
1831-1836	Expedition on the HMS *Beagle*
1838-1841	Secretary of Geological Society
1839	Published *The Journal of a Naturalist*
1839	Married Emma Wedgwood, with whom he later had ten children
1840	Published *Zoology of the Voyage of the Beagle*
1842	Published *The Structure & Distribution of Coral Reef*
1842	Began writing *On the Origin of Species by Natural Selection*
1851-1853	Published *Monograph on the Cirripedia*
1858	Essays of Wallace and Darwin were discovered to contain similar views
1859	Published *On the Origin of Species by Natural Selection*
1862	Published *Fertilization of Orchids*
1868	Published *Variation of Animals & Plants Under Domestication*
1871	Published *The Descent of Man & Selection in Relation to Sex*
1872	Published *The Expression of Emotions in Man & Animals*
1876	Published *Effects of Cross and Self-Fertilization in the Vegetable Kingdom*
1882	Died on April 19 at the age of 73

GLOSSARY

Adapted Changed to fit in with.

Ancestor Family member who lived long ago and is now dead.

Barometer Instrument to measure air pressure and forecast the weather.

Barque Sailing ship with three masts. The two front masts carried square sails; the back mast carried fore-and-aft sails.

Bilges Space at the bottom of a ship's hold.

Bolas Wooden balls on ropes, used by South American cowboys to catch wild animals by tripping them.

Brig Sailing ship with two masts carrying square sails.

Charts Maps of seas and coasts.

Cholera Dangerous disease, carried by polluted water, that kills many of its victims.

Civilians People who do not belong to armed forces.

Clinometer Instrument to measure slopes.

Curing Rubbing with salt or other chemicals to preserve.

Draughtsmen Artists who are skilled at technical drawings.

Embryo A fertilized egg in the early stages of developing into a human or animal.

Emigrants People who leave one country to settle in another.

Evolution The scientific theory that all life on earth is descended from a single common ancestor.

Extinct No longer living; died out.

Fore-and-aft Sails carried parallel to a ship's deck, pointing towards the prow and the stern.

Fossils The remains of creatures that lived long ago, preserved in stone.

Gauchos South American cowboys.

Geological To do with geology.

Geology The science of rocks, minerals and the earth.

Helmsman Sailor who steers a ship.

Hold Cargo compartment in a ship's hull.

Hygrometer Instrument used for measuring moisture.

Imported Brought from a foreign land.

Latitude The distance North or South of the equator, measured in degrees.

Lava Molten (melted) rock that pours from an erupting volcano.

Longitude The distance East or West from Greenwich, London, expressed in degrees.

Lieutenant Junior officer.

Malady Sickness.

Marines Soldiers who fight at sea.

Mast Tall pole that supports sails on ships.

Microscope Scientific instrument that allows someone to see the details of very small objects or living things.

Mizzen mast Mast near the stern (back) of the ship, which carried fore-and-aft sails.

Molten Melted.

Muskets Guns that fire small metal balls.

Natural Selection Darwin's theory that only those living things best suited to their environment will survive.

Navigate Steer a course.

On reserve Ready and waiting to be of use.

Parasitic Animals or plants that live off other living creatures.

Pitch Sticky black tar.

Plot To mark a planned journey on a chart.

Prehensile Strong and flexible. Able to be used like an extra hand.

Prow The front of a ship.

Rudder Large paddle at the stern (back) of a ship. Used to steer it.

Seaworthy Watertight and strong enough to survive a sea voyage.

Sloop Small, fast sailing ship with one mast and triangular sails.

Specimens Examples of rocks and wildlife.

Spirit Alcohol Used to stop dead creatures from rotting.

Square-rigged With sails carried at right-angles (90 degrees) to a mast.

Stays Ropes used to support masts on sailing ships.

Stern Back end of a ship.

Survey Examining and recording details of land and coasts.

Taxidermy Preserving dead creatures by curing their skins and stuffing them to retain their appearance.

Teredo worms Worms that live in warm seas. They eat and destroy wood.

INDEX